Encounter with God

God

with

- a collection of prayers and meditations

by Dennis Wrigley

photography and design by Tony Hill

Published by Word for Life Trust, The House of Bread, Ross Road,
Christchurch, Glos GL16 7NS. All enquiries to the publishers e-mail: resources@wflt.org.
or the author at Maranatha Community, 102 Irlam Road, Flixton, Manchester M41 6JT
e-mail: info@maranathacommunity.org.uk

ISBN 1-903577-23-3

Distributed by:
New Wine Ministries, 22 Arun Business Park, Bognor Regis PO22 9SX
e-mail: newwine@xalt.co.uk

Unless otherwise stated, all scripture quotations are from
the Holy Bible, New International Version, copyright 1973, 1978, 1984
by the INTERNATIONAL BIBLE SOCIETY.
Used by permission of Hodder and Stoughton Ltd.

British Library Cataloguing Data
A catalogue record of this book is available from the British Library.
All rights reserved.

Scroll with each scripture by Sister Susan Norbury - used with her permission.
Scriptures selected by Sister Elizabeth Tuttle PBVM.
Both are acknowledged with thanks by the author and photographer.

Printed in China

Contents

Foreword

———

by Professor the Lord Alton of Liverpool

Alfred, Lord Tennyson, famously wrote that "more things are wrought by prayer than this world dreams of." I also love the thought, captured by Saint Augustine, that we "should pray as if the entire outcome depends upon God and work as if the entire outcome depends upon us."

In their different ways, Tennyson and Saint Augustine are admonishing us not to place all our reliance in our own efforts but to learn the gentle art of sharing with God the things that challenge and worry us.

In this short anthology, Dennis Wrigley, drawing on the deep prayer life of the Maranatha Community, shares with us some prayers that will animate our own prayer lives and help us to connect more easily to our Father and Maker.

Liverpool, UK   1st March 2005

by The Rev'd. Elizabeth Brazell

As Director of Word for Life Trust, I want to thank Dennis Wrigley and Tony Hill for asking us to publish this beautiful and inspiring book.

We have already used many of the prayers here at our healing centre in the Forest of Dean for retreats and quiet days, and have seen the Lord touch, bless, heal and guide through the Holy Spirit's anointing, realised in the praying of these meditations. Thank you, Tony, for the illustrations so prayerfully and imaginatively collected. Thank you, Dennis, for listening to God's heartbeat of love and writing as He led you.

There is an accompanying CD with many of these prayers and others - we commend it to our readers. May the Lord bless you greatly as you read on......

Gloucestershire, UK   7th March 2005

1

Introduction

Dennis Wrigley, the author, writes:

These prayers flow from my own personal journey, with its joys and sadnesses. They also flow from the life of the Maranatha Community with which I have been involved for twenty-five years.

The first prayer, 'Shalom', was given to me early on a Sunday morning by the Lord, on a deserted coastland of a Greek island, as I prayed with Sheila, my wife. Since then this prayer has been printed and used by thousands of different people all over the world. We are constantly encouraged by the messages we receive from those who have experienced healing, blessings and conversion through using 'Shalom' and other prayers in this collection. The prayers have blessed people facing personal crisis, experiencing bereavement, suffering the pain of broken relationships, serving prison sentences or on remand, and from those suffering sicknesses, abuse, drug or alcohol addictions. Letters from these people always contain good news and some report dramatic healing and transformation. Sometimes young people write, full of hope, as they are discovering a dynamic and living relationship with God through these prayers.

Maranatha is a nation-wide movement of Christians drawn from every tradition and bound together within the love of Christ. It is a healing Community with a great emphasis upon prayer and listening to God. It is not a church but a resource committed to support individuals and churches. Maranatha's silent retreats and days of quietness have led many into a deeper relationship with God and a very close personal experience of the real presence of Christ. In a world torn by division we have been led into a real unity with each other and with the Lord. In a world bursting with pain and sickness we have been led into deep healing. In an unbelieving world we have been led to a new meeting with God and the renewal of a living faith. More recently, God has called us, as a Community, to simplicity and spiritual poverty. Therefore our endeavour is to live and proclaim the simple Gospel with an increasing sense of urgency.

I hope that readers of 'Encounter with God' who, like myself, live in a noisy and confused world, will be refreshed and will hear the still small voice of God whose mighty Spirit is love and truth. May the Lord bless, encourage and meet with each one of you.

.. and Tony Hill, the photographer adds:

What a privilege it has been to be asked to illustrate and present this collection of Dennis' prayers for publication. Two years in the making, from very small beginnings – a chance remark, an unexpected encounter, through many extraordinary "God-incidences", this book developed and grew, becoming an incredible journey into areas undreamt of with Jesus every step of the way.

The mechanics were simple. Pray each prayer, sometimes many times, always asking the Lord to "speak His background" into it. And listen. Again and again I have stood amazed at the way He has led me to an appropriate photograph, and then how He has shown how the text could be flowed into it, in ways far beyond my understanding. Many questions remain unanswered. Why this? Why now? Why me? Why just these prayers? One thing I do know. I have seen the Lord at work. In every word, in every prayer, in every picture I have encountered afresh the risen Lord Jesus. It is my hope and prayer that you too will find Him here.

3

The Prayers

Shalom

I come as myself.
Just as I am.
This moment.
My feelings,
my fears,
my joys, my sadnesses.
You see me as I really am.
You know me
through and through.
You see all, all that I am,
or ever have been.

Every experience in my life is laid before You.
Every image I have seen,
each touch, each sensation,
every word I have ever heard or spoken,
each word, each idea,
each thought which is imprinted in my soul
and is known to You.
You know me better than my closest friend.
You know me better than I know myself.

You know...
and because of who I am
and in spite of what I am - You love me.
I am of inestimable value to You.
You love me through and through.
Nothing, nobody can remove me from Your love.
Nothing, nobody can separate me
from Your love or Your presence.

You knew me
at the moment of my creation
and even then You loved me.
You knew me and loved me in my mother's womb.
My nature was known to You.
You called me by my name,
You held me in Your arms,
You embraced me,
You breathed upon me;
You gave me Your life and Your love.
You watched over me
from my earliest childhood.

You were present at all times and in all places,
my unseen playmate, schoolmate, workmate,
my unseen guest at every meal.
You shared in every encounter.
You watched over me silently
even in the long hours of the night.
You shared in every journey
You travelled with me.
You were at the beginning of each journey.
You were my companion on the way.

Without You I lose my way;
my journey has no purpose.
I become exhausted on the way.
But You are my Alpha and Omega.
You are my way .
You are the way itself, the Way of Life.

So Lord I lay before You my life,
 all my yesterdays,
  my todays and tomorrows.
   I praise and thank You for Your presence in my life.
   I lift up in gratitude all the goodness and all the joy.

I now offer You all my hurts,
my bruises, my rejections,
I offer You all those things of which I am ashamed,
what I have said, and done, and thought,
all that has brought hurt to You and to others.
Lord pour Your cleansing streams of living water
all over me.
Make the parched deserts of my being spring to life.
Refresh me, renew me.

Lord breathe on me afresh now
 and I will receive Your life.
  Lord reach out and touch me
   and I will receive Your healing.
    Empty me utterly of all the rubbish within me.
     This moment, Lord,
       take away all distractions, all temptations,
        all evil thoughts and desires.
         Remove from me all my anxiety,
          take away every hidden fear.
           Help me to know
             that Your perfect love
              casts out all fear.

Bring me now into the deep silence of Your presence.
        I give You my body
    and ask that it may become Your dwelling place;
 this moment may every part of my being be at peace.
            Let my heartbeat
       be in harmony with Your heartbeat;
        let every part of my body
         be filled with Your Spirit.
           Take each blood vessel,
        take every part of my nervous system,
       take each muscle, each organ, each cell.
            Fill me now
          with Your stillness,
     with the reality of Your living presence.

  Help me now to pray - even without words.
    Help me to pray with my breathing,
  to breathe in of Your love and Your peace,
    to breathe out of my pain and sadness,
  to breathe in of Your cleansing and forgiveness,
     to breathe out of my guilt and impurity.
So in my breathing may my body and soul be at one with You,
        in harmony with You,
          at ease with You.

   May I be still and know that You are God.
      May I be still and know
          that You are
    the Lord who brings healing.

6

Help me to hear Your still, small voice, Lord Jesus.
May I now hear Your words - 'Peace, be still'.
May all my storms subside
as I accept Your real presence.
As I kneel before You
I give You my heart and all my emotions,
all my deepest feelings that lie hidden within me.
I give You my stillness
but I also give You the turbulence,
the cross-currents of my life,
my feelings of failure and rejection.
I give You every relationship,
every situation in my life,
all my reactions,
all my outbursts of joy and of anger,
all my moments of elation and despair.
Lord I give You my intellect.
I lay before You all my frail thoughts and ideas.
I give You all my searching and striving,
my grasping after truth.
I give You all my ignorance and confusion,
I give You all my questions and doubts.
I acknowledge You to be truth,
truth in its entirety,
total truth in all its purity,
the Truth which can set me free,
in my body, my mind and my spirit.,
free from all the bondage,
free from all the lies and deceit of the world,
free
from my own selfishness and pride and greed.

Break the chains
which hold me back Lord,
fling open the door of my prison
that I may pass
from the darkness of this world - my world
and walk out
into the bright light of Your presence.
Father, may I now feel
the radiance of Your love upon my life.
May I feel the warmth
of Your fatherly love upon me, Your child
trusting, depending, loving.
Help me to know what joy my response brings to You.
Give me the grace in my weakness to cry
'Abba', Father.
Help me to know that beneath me
are Your everlasting arms bearing me up.

Lord Jesus, be the Lord of my life.
Be the Lord of my thoughts and feelings,
my memories and hopes.
I accept Your authority
over everything I have been, am or will be.
I bow down before You.
As I see You on Your Cross
held down by cruel nails
I see Your arms stretched out
seeking to embrace the whole world,
seeking to embrace me,
seeking to love, seeking to forgive,
seeking to make whole.

I praise You -
that You died for me.
Help me to know
that because Your love for me was so great
I too must love myself.
I must recognise
my great worth to You.

Holy Spirit, source of all truth, giver of power,
come upon me now
as gently as a dove
or like tongues of living fire,
as quietly as a summer breeze
or as a mighty roaring wind.
Come and dwell within me.
Enable me now to do those things which
before were impossible.

Unworthy as I am, Holy Spirit of the living God,
give me those gifts which I can use
to Your honour and glory
that I may show forth Your fruit
even in my life.

Glory be to You Father.
Glory be to You Lord Jesus Christ.
Glory be to You Holy Spirit.
Amen.

We have seen his glory,
the glory of the One and Only,
who came from the Father,
full of grace and truth.

John 1 : 14

I behold Your glory
and am at once made blind.
My imperfect self
shrivels up
when faced with Your perfection.
My impurities
are laid bare
by the brightness of Your purity.
My finite self
is overwhelmed
by Your infinity.
The dross of my life
is consumed by Your refining fire.

So when I look towards You, my Lord,
and Lord of all
and turn my eyes
upon Your majesty and might
and seek to gaze upon Your beauty
I am at once diminished,
laid low,
stripped naked in my poverty
and littleness.

Yet at the same time
I am raised up
to my full humanity,
redeemed,
cleansed,
sanctified,
and free.

Your Glory

"Come with me by yourselves to a quiet place
and get some rest."

Mark 6 : 31

Your Gift

You bid me leave
my busyness,
the structures which
imprison me,
the plans
the schemes
the ticking clock,
the noise
the words
the instant shock.
You lead me
to the desert
bereft of every load
no rushing, pushing,
striving, seeking,
just the timeless
eternity
of Your presence
and a perennial
youthfulness
which is Your gift.

To the only God our Saviour,
be glory, majesty, power and authority,
through Jesus Christ our Lord, before all ages,
now and for evermore!
Amen.

Jude 25

Awesome God

You are
You have been
You will be,
beyond time,
beyond space.

Without beginning
without end.
Infinite
in power,
in knowledge.

Creator of all,
Giver of life,
perfect in Your ways.
Absolute truth,
limitless love.

Glorious Lord,
ruler over all,
source of wisdom.
Ground of being,
awesome in majesty,
the great 'I am',
before whom
I needs must
prostrate myself
in amazement,
and gaze upon You
in awe
and wonder
and wordless silence.

Jesus stood and said in a loud voice,
"If anyone is thirsty, let him come to me and drink.
Whoever believes in me, as the Scripture has said,
streams of living water will flow from within him."

John 7 : 37

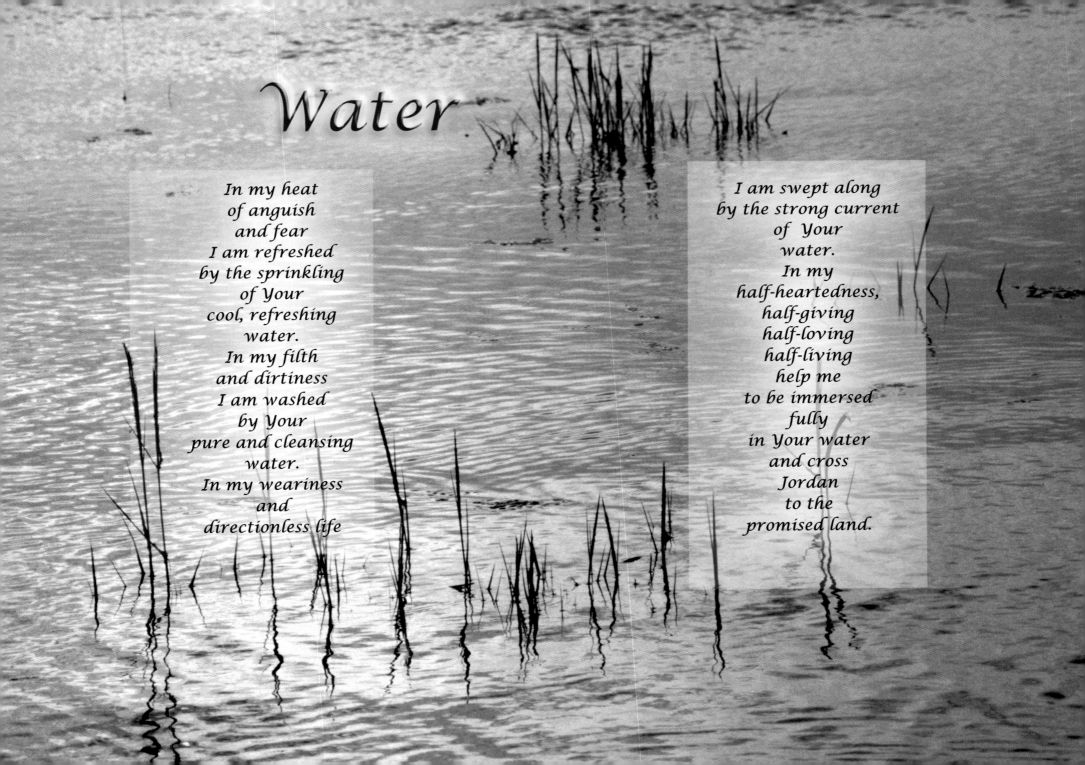

Water

In my heat
of anguish
and fear
I am refreshed
by the sprinkling
of Your
cool, refreshing
water.
In my filth
and dirtiness
I am washed
by Your
pure and cleansing
water.
In my weariness
and
directionless life

I am swept along
by the strong current
of Your
water.
In my
half-heartedness,
half-giving
half-loving
half-living
help me
to be immersed
fully
in Your water
and cross
Jordan
to the
promised land.

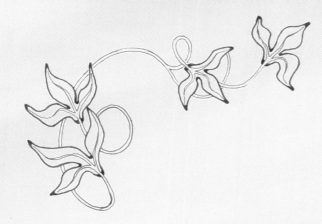

Be still before the Lord, all mankind, because
He has roused himself from his holy dwelling.

Zechariah 2 : 13

You are Here

Alone with You
I kneel in awe
and silence
Lord.

Mighty Creator
all space is Your habitation,
yet
You are here
in this place
now.

Immortal Ruler of the years
all time
is filled with Your presence,
yet
You are here - and near
this moment.

All-seeing and all-knowing God
all truth flows from You,
and
You see and know me as I am.

All-loving and
all-caring Father
compassion flows
from You,
and
You love and care for me
as I am.

Apart from You
I have no security.
Absent from You
I am lost.
Touch me, hold me,
breathe on me
and I will live forever
in Christ, Your Son,
my Saviour.

Ask and it will be given........
seek and you will find;
knock and the door will be opened to you.

Matthew 7 : 7

His Abundance

I reach out
into the dark
and find there
the warm, strong grasp
of the hand of God.
I falter and stumble
and am at once
raised up
in loving arms.
I seek, and
- joy of joys -
I find.
I knock
and the door
is opened wide.
I ask;
He gives in bounty
all I need.
In darkest prison
I cry out -

- and He gently leads me
into the light
of His presence,
locks shattered,
chains destroyed,
tightest bonds all cut away.
I come to Him
in blindness,
and now
receive my sight.
My tears turn into laughter,
my night
into glorious day.
Food for my hunger
is given,
and warmth
for my coldness of heart.
In abundance
my God provides
for me.

I have set the Lord always before me.
Because he is at my right hand
I shall not be shaken.

Psalm 16 : 8

All my Days

From the silence
of the heights
I look
down
on the
winding
path
of my life,
and in my solitary
stillness
I catch a glimpse
and taste the flavour
of rich encounters,
moments of joys
and sadnesses
long past,
visions and echoes
of people,
places,
and circumstances,
each of value
and some
of greatest worth.

And seeing,
I recognise
Your hand
upon my days,
Your presence,
never changing,
within
my ever-changing life.
I see not where
the path will lead
in coming days,
but know
that all is in Your care,
and that all
that is past - and yet to be
is vibrantly alive.
For the One
whose sameness
then, and now,
and for eternity
is the Rock
of my strength,
my refuge
and salvation,
and against this Rock
the storms of time
beat all in vain.

From the fulness of his grace
we have all received
one blessing after another.

John 1 : 16

Encounter

The brief encounter,
the exchanged glance,
the passing word -
- received or given.
The momentary touch,
the glad surprise,
the sudden glimpse
of paradise -
all these are gifts
from the One
in whom there is
no chance coincidence,
with whom our every breath
and act and thought
are intertwined
with order
and purpose
and the love
which is the currency
of life.

You will fill me with joy in your presence, with eternal pleasures at your right hand.

Psalm 16 : 11b

Silence
beyond all silence.
Stillness
beyond all stillness,
heights
and depths
of motionlessness,
filled with
the peace,
the formlessness,
the awesome
nearness
of Your presence
- this the ultimate reality,
the very breath
of God.

The Breath of God

I will not forget you! See I have engraved you
on the palms of my hands.

Isaiah 49 : 15b-16

People are Gifts

The gifts You give me
are people, Lord.
Gifts for a moment
or for the years of my life,
all from You,
reflections of You
if I but look.
Each with a dignity,
a worth,
imprinted with Your hand,
Your image clearly carved upon their being.
Behind each eye, each mask,
within each package,
beyond all hiding
and all camouflage,
a precious one
to be handled
with the greatest care
and sensitivity -
a gift beyond all price,
never to be damaged
or rejected
or abused,
- a gift unlike all other gifts.
A gift to love
protect and cherish
with wonder and with awe;
A gift of God.

There is a time for everything,
and a season for every activity under heaven.

Ecclesiastes 3 : 1

Fallen Leaves

The leaves have fallen,
the ground is still,
the trees reach out and up,
motionless.
Yet in their dignity
expectant,
standing very still
in the crisp air
against the sharp
and steely sky,
nostalgically recalling
the gentle summer days
and now awaiting
the frost and wind,
snow and rain
of winter
without which
there can be no spring,
no coming of new life.

Help me to be part of
that stillness,
and to know
that spring
is not far away,
that the brief
soft flutter
of a lonely bird
is but a portent
- a preparation
of Your coming -
a statement
that I must be still
and know
and feel
that
You are God.

Exalt the Lord our God and
worship at His footstool;
he is holy.

Psalm 99 : 5

To see You
my gaze must be
steadfast
fixed
and tranquil.
My awareness
of myself,
my needs
my feelings
my desires
must diminish
and die away
as I am overwhelmed
with Your Glory,
Your perfection,
Your limitless love,
Your all-consuming beauty,
and I am utterly lost
in You,
filled with awe,
making no requests,
expressing nothing of self,
simply adoring
the One
who is my all in all.

Adoration

Be still, and know that I am God.

Psalm 46 : 10

Calm Delight

I allow
the noise of the world
to fade away
into the far distance,
and the soft breeze
of the breath of God
to blow in gentleness
upon my life,
bringing refreshment
and a sense
of well-being
and calm delight
to my troubled soul,
and in the quietness
my Lord tells me
in simplicity,
Be still,
and then I know
that He is God.

I will turn the desert into pools of water,
and the parched ground into springs.

Isaiah 41 : 18b

God of the Desert

Absent
from the chaotic noise
of an unreal world,
entering the
desert solitude
and stillness,
I wait upon
the God
who comes
to disturb me
with His
all-pervading
peace,
with His penetrating
truth,
with His
ominous, awesome,
all-knowing
presence.

He plumbs the depths
of my being,
revealing the hidden,
touching the untouched,
and in the
raw simplicity
of this
wilderness encounter,
this wrestling
of the spirit,
I am set free,
with opened eyes,
and unstopped ears,
to meet Him
on His mountain top,
to breathe in
of the freshness
and the purity
of His being,
knowing something
of the mystery
of His love.

O Lord, you have searched me and you know me........
You perceive my thoughts from afar.

Psalm 139 : 1 and 2b

You
are nearer
to me
than I am
to myself.
You have
searched me
and know me,
and You discern
all my thoughts.
My roots
go deep
into Your depths
for You
are the ground
of my being,
nourishing,
upholding,
enfolding me,
yet ever
drawing me up
to the
blinding light
of Your
radiant Glory.

The Ground of my Being

The Son is the radiance of God's glory
and the exact representation of his being,
sustaining all things by his powerful word.

Hebrews 1 : 3

In His Presence

From a position
of not moving,
not stirring,
not striving,
not articulating
words, ideas and concepts,
from this position
of total silence,
total inactivity,
saying nothing,
doing nothing,
just breathing
I look with utter submission
and adoration
at my Lord.

Consumed
by His purity,
overwhelmed
by His love,
blinded
by His radiance,
filled with awe,
desiring simply
to remain
in His presence,
to give Him
my total attention,
to focus
my whole being
on the One who is,
always has been
the centre and source
of my whole life -
Jesus.

Whoever loses his life for my sake will find it.

Matthew 10 : 39b

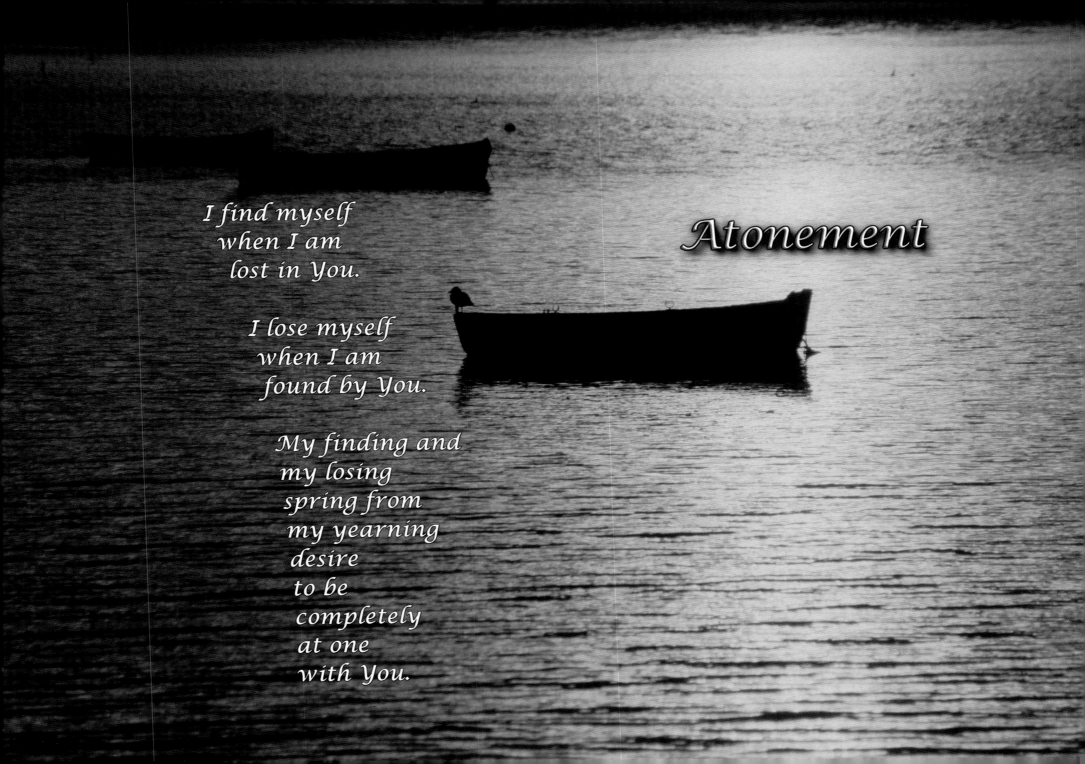

Atonement

I find myself
when I am
lost in You.

I lose myself
when I am
found by You.

My finding and
my losing
spring from
my yearning
desire
to be
completely
at one
with You.

I pray that you,
being rooted and established in love,
may have power....... to grasp how wide and
long and high and deep is the love of Christ.

Ephesians 3 :17

The evidence
of Your presence
is everywhere.
Your breath
is upon my life.
You hover over me;
You lay Your hand upon
me,
You hold me
in your arms.
You warm my heart;
You are deep within me,
the very ground
of my being.
You are more real
than reality.
You are beyond
all words,
beyond all images
and definitions.
You are beyond,
yet very present
here and now,
in Christ.

Your Presence

....God exalted him (Jesus) to the highest place and gave him the name that is above every name.

Philippians 2 : 9

I come to the One
who has the Name
above all names.
I bow before Him
for never have I known
such purity,
such manifest truth.
Here is the One
who towers over all,
in might and majesty,
in awesome tenderness
and peace
beyond all words,
beyond compare.
Alone.
Unique.
Jesus.

I come

to Jesus

We love because he first loved us.

1 John 4 : 19

I come,
in awesome silence
into Your presence.
No words,
no pleading,
no concepts or designs.
I encounter You
in this stillness
which settles,
deep
within my soul.
Beyond all time
and thought.
I wait upon You,
I rest beneath Your shadow.
I feel Your breath
upon my life
and discover anew
that it is not I
who come to You,
but You
who come to me,
and in Your coming
You commune
with Your Spirit within me
and I am at once
made whole
and all
is well.

The God who Comes

Not by might nor by power,
but by my Spirit,
says the Lord Almighty.

Zechariah 4 : 6

How?

How
can I love
the unlovable?

How can I forgive
the unforgivable?

How can I touch
the untouchable?

How can I be close
to the sinner -
yet be separate
from the sin?

How can I be in the world
-yet not be of it?

How can I walk
the dangerous ways
of Jesus?

Not by might
not by power
but
by My Spirit
says the Lord.

Jesus said,
"I have come that they may have life
and have it to the full."

John 10 : 10

The rising sap,
the bursting bud,
the fresh green shoot,
the bird on the wind,
gurgling mountain streams,
the urgent chatter
of little children.
All these tell me
of the gift of life
in all its abundance
which the Lord pours forth
upon all creatures
and all creation
with joy
and even the ripple
of laughter.
Why then
with all this colour
and the prospect
of vibrant living,
overflowing
with the excitement
of newness,
why do we choose the death
of a Godless life,
spurning the giver,
choosing darkness
in place of life?

Why?

Heal me, O Lord, and I shall be healed.

Jeremiah 17 : 14

At a time of Need

Lord,
You have made me
and my life
is in Your safe hands.
I do not need to fear
because I am cradled
in Your love.
When I allow You
to dwell within my heart
I live in perfect safety,
and Your Peace
enters my being.

Therefore I give you
my mind
my emotions
my body
my feelings.
Take them, Lord,
bless them
transform them
heal them.

Go to the root of all my disorders.
Touch those parts of me
which hurt -
my pains, discomforts
and unease.

Touch me and make me whole.
Come
to my weaknesses
and bring Your strength.
Come to my restlessness
and bring Your stillness.

Come
and reveal to me
Your goodness
and Your mercy,
and in Your coming
reveal to me
Your nearness,
that I may know
that I am not alone,
and that
moment by moment
You bear my sorrows,
share my joys
and will never leave me
nor forsake me,
that You will pour out
the richness of Your healing
upon me,
this child
You know so well
and love so dearly.

Taste and see that the Lord is good.

Psalm 34 : 8

The Gift of this Moment

This moment will not return;
it is a precious gift
to me, for all eternity.
Here, now
I can savour this gift,
receive it, enjoy it, use it,
but I can wish it away,
throw it away,
discard it......
because I am tired,
impatient,
anxious,
depressed,
because I am too busy
recalling the past
plotting the future,
hastily dismissing this instant,
yet I will never pass this way again.
it will be cast in the stone of time.
What is there in this transient moment
which I can fill with life?

Why have I been brought
to this point of time
which is filled with such potential?

Giver of this gift
I ask You to make it eternally rich
to awaken in me its infinite potential.
Help me
to begin to see with Your eyes,
to begin to hear with Your ears,
to begin to breathe Your breath,
to begin to be filled with Your life
and Your love;
to awaken fully
to what You are saying
and doing
just now.

Make this moment
a time of joy,
of freedom,
exhilaration,
and even ecstasy
here and now.

May I taste and see
how good You are
and in my refreshment
give You glory and praise.

Peace I leave with you;
my peace I give you.
I do not give to you as the world gives.

John 14 : 27

Your Peace

In my breathing
Peace.
In my feeling
Peace.
In my being
Peace.
In my thinking
Peace.
In my speaking
Peace.
In my doing
Peace.
In my travelling
Peace.
In my sleeping
Peace.
In my whole being
- the Peace
far beyond my understanding
for it is the Peace
which is of God
and which is God.

If you would like further information about the Christian faith or an introduction to a local church, please contact:

Word for Life Trust, The House of Bread, Ross Road, Christchurch, Gloucestershire GL16 7NS
Tel: +44(0)1594 837744, Fax: +44(0)1594 837742, e-mail: wflt@wflt.org
Charity Registration No: 1071313

or

The Maranatha Community Trust, 102, Irlam Road, Flixton, Manchester, M41 6JT
Tel: +(0)0161 748 4858, Fax: +44(0)0161 747 7379
e-mail: info@maranathacommunity.org.uk
Registered Charity No: 327627